SMALL BUSINESS BOOKKEEPING FOR NEWBIES

Calculate Your Way from Small Business into BIG BUSINESS

SMART2GO TRAINING®

SMART2GO TRAINING® 2024. All rights reserved. No part of this book may be reproduced or transmitted in any form or by any means, electronic or mechanical, including photocopying, recording or by any information storage and retrieval system without written permission from the author, except for the inclusion of brief quotations in a review.

Disclaimer/Terms of Use

In no way is it legal to reproduce, duplicate, or transmit any part of this book in either electronic means or in printed format.

Recording of this publication is strictly prohibited and any other storage of this document is not allowed unless with written permission from the publisher. All rights reserved.

The information provided herein is stated to be truthful and consistent, in that any liability, in terms of inattention or otherwise, by any usage or abuse of any policies, processes, or directions contained within is the solitary and utter responsibility of the recipient reader. Under no circumstances will any legal responsibility or blame be held against the publisher for any reparation, damages, or monetary loss due to the information herein, either directly or indirectly.

Respective authors own all copyrights not held by the publisher. The information herein is offered for information and education purposes solely and is universal as so. The information is without contract or any type of guaranteed assurance.

Contents

Mastering Cash Flow for Your Small Business: A Comprehensive Guide 7
    The Importance of Cash Flow Management 7
    Strategies for Managing Cash Flow 8
    Distinguishing Cash Flow from Profit 9
    Tools for Cash Flow Management 9

Understanding Working Capital: The Lifeblood of Business Operations 11
    What is Working Capital? 11
    Importance of Working Capital 11
    Calculating Working Capital 12
    Example of Working Capital Calculation 13
    Managing Working Capital 13
    Tips to Improve Working Capital 14

Understanding Liquidity Ratios: Key Indicators of Financial Health 15
    What is a Liquidity Ratio? 15
    Importance of Liquidity Ratios 15
    Calculating Liquidity Ratios 16

Understanding Current Ratio: A Key Indicator of Financial Health 19

Understanding the Quick Ratio: A Crucial Measure of Financial Liquidity 23

Understanding the Cash Ratio: A Critical Measure of Liquidity 27

Understanding the Debt Ratio: Measuring Financial Leverage and Risk 31

Understanding Gross Margin: A Key Indicator of Business Profitability 35

Understanding Profit Margin: A Comprehensive Indicator of Business Success 39

Understanding Return on Equity (ROE): A Key Indicator of Shareholder Value 43

Mastering Cash Flow for Your Small Business: A Comprehensive Guide

Effective financial management is a cornerstone of any successful business, especially for small business owners. One of the most critical aspects of this is understanding and managing cash flow. Cash flow, which refers to the movement of money in and out of your business, is essential for ensuring that you can cover your expenses, invest in growth opportunities, and maintain financial stability. This guide will delve into the basics of cash flow accounting and provide practical advice to help you manage your business finances effectively.

Defining Cash Flow

Cash flow represents the lifeblood of your business, indicating how cash enters and exits your enterprise. There are two primary types of cash flow:

1. **Positive Cash Flow**: This occurs when the cash inflows exceed the cash outflows, signaling a financially healthy business capable of covering its expenses and potentially investing in future growth.

2. **Negative Cash Flow**: This happens when cash outflows surpass cash inflows. While it can be manageable in the short term, prolonged negative cash flow can jeopardize the business's financial stability.

The Importance of Cash Flow Management

Understanding cash flow is crucial for several reasons:

- **Operational Efficiency**: Ensures that you have sufficient funds to cover day-to-day expenses such as rent, utilities, salaries, and supplier payments.

- **Growth Opportunities**: Positive cash flow provides the financial flexibility to invest in new projects, expand operations, and hire additional staff.

- **Financial Health**: Proper cash flow management reduces the need for borrowing, lowers the risk of insolvency, and provides a buffer against unforeseen financial challenges.

Components of Cash Flow

Cash flow is categorized into three main components:

1. **Operating Activities**: Cash generated or expended from core business operations, including sales revenue and operating expenses.

2. **Investing Activities**: Cash used for or generated from investments in the business, such as purchasing equipment or selling assets.

3. **Financing Activities**: Cash related to borrowing or repaying loans, issuing shares, or other financial activities.

Constructing a Cash Flow Statement

A cash flow statement is a financial document that provides a summary of cash inflows and outflows over a specific period. Here's how to create one:

1. **Identify Cash Inflows**: List all sources of cash entering the business, such as sales revenue, loans, and other income streams.

2. **Identify Cash Outflows**: List all cash expenditures, including rent, utilities, salaries, loan repayments, and other expenses.

3. **Calculate Net Cash Flow**: Subtract total cash outflows from total cash inflows to determine the net cash flow. A positive figure indicates positive cash flow, while a negative figure indicates negative cash flow.

In this example, the shop has a positive net cash flow of $5,000 for the month.

Strategies for Managing Cash Flow

Effective cash flow management is vital for the sustainability and growth of your business. Here are several strategies to help you manage your cash flow:

1. **Regular Monitoring**: Consistently track and update your cash flow statement to stay informed about your financial status and identify potential issues early.

2. **Forecasting**: Project future cash inflows and outflows to anticipate and plan for upcoming financial needs and avoid unexpected shortfalls.

3. **Expense Control**: Analyze your expenses and look for opportunities to reduce costs, such as negotiating better terms with suppliers or finding more cost-effective solutions.

4. **Accelerate Receivables**: Encourage customers to pay invoices promptly by offering discounts for early payments or utilizing online payment systems for convenience.

5. **Maintain a Cash Reserve**: Establish a reserve fund to cover unexpected expenses and provide a financial cushion during lean periods.

Distinguishing Cash Flow from Profit

It's essential to distinguish between cash flow and profit, as both are critical but represent different aspects of your business's financial health:

- **Cash Flow**: Refers to the actual movement of cash in and out of your business, reflecting the liquidity available to meet immediate and short-term obligations.
- **Profit**: Represents the financial gain after all expenses have been deducted from total revenue, indicating the overall profitability of your business over a specific period.

A business can be profitable but still experience cash flow problems if there's a delay in receiving payments from customers. For example, high sales might lead to profit, but if customers delay their payments, the business might struggle to meet its immediate financial obligations.

Tools for Cash Flow Management

Several tools and software are available to assist you in managing your cash flow efficiently:

- **Accounting Software**: Programs like QuickBooks, Xero, and FreshBooks help track cash flow, generate financial statements, and manage expenses.
- **Spreadsheets**: Microsoft Excel and Google Sheets can be used to create and update custom cash flow statements.
- **Cash Flow Management Apps**: Specialized apps like Float, Pulse, and Cash Flow Frog are designed to help small business owners monitor and manage cash flow.

Mastering cash flow management is crucial for the success and sustainability of your small business. By regularly tracking your cash inflows and outflows, creating detailed cash flow statements, and utilizing effective management strategies, you can ensure your business remains financially healthy and prepared for growth. Remember, positive cash flow allows you to cover your operational expenses, invest in new opportunities, and maintain a financial buffer against unexpected challenges. Prioritize cash flow management, and your business will be well-positioned to thrive in the competitive market.

Understanding Working Capital: The Lifeblood of Business Operations

By learning how to calculate, interpret and use financial ratios you will understand how to assess the financial strength of a firm, to analyze management effectiveness in employing capital, and how solvent and profitable is the company.

Working capital is a fundamental concept in financial management, crucial for the day-to-day functioning of a business. It represents the short-term liquidity available to a company and its ability to meet its immediate obligations. Understanding and managing working capital effectively can ensure a business remains solvent, can invest in its operations, and can respond to unforeseen financial challenges. This section reveals what working capital is, its importance, and the formula to calculate it.

What is Working Capital?

Working capital, often referred to as net working capital (NWC), is the difference between a company's current assets and current liabilities. Current assets include assets that are expected to be converted into cash within a year, such as cash and cash equivalents, accounts receivable, and inventory. Current liabilities are obligations the company must pay within the same period, including accounts payable, short-term debt, and other similar liabilities.

This simple formula provides a snapshot of a company's short-term financial health. Positive working capital indicates that a company has enough short-term assets to cover its short-term liabilities, whereas negative working capital suggests potential liquidity issues.

Importance of Working Capital

Working capital plays a pivotal role in the financial stability and operational efficiency of a business. Here are several reasons why working capital is important:

1. **Liquidity Management**: Adequate working capital ensures that a business can meet its short-term obligations, such as paying suppliers and employees, thereby maintaining smooth operations.

2. **Operational Efficiency**: Sufficient working capital allows a company to invest in its operations, purchase inventory, and take advantage of bulk purchasing discounts. It also provides the flexibility to cope with unexpected expenses or opportunities.

3. **Financial Health**: Positive working capital is a sign of good financial health, indicating that a business can sustain its operations without relying excessively on external financing. This

can enhance the company's creditworthiness and make it easier to secure loans or attract investors.

4. **Growth and Expansion**: With adequate working capital, a business can fund its growth initiatives, such as expanding product lines, entering new markets, or investing in marketing campaigns, without straining its resources.

5. **Risk Management**: Maintaining an optimal level of working capital helps a business manage risks associated with cash flow fluctuations, economic downturns, or changes in market conditions.

Calculating Working Capital

The formula to calculate working capital is straightforward:

Working Capital = Current Assets – Current Liabilities

To understand how this formula works in practice, let's break down the components:

1. **Current Assets**: These are assets that a company expects to convert into cash within a year. They include:
    - Cash and cash equivalents: Money available immediately.
    - Accounts receivable: Money owed by customers for sales made on credit.
    - Inventory: Goods available for sale.
    - Short-term investments: Investments that can be liquidated within a year.
    - Prepaid expenses: Payments made in advance for services to be received within a year.

2. **Current Liabilities**: These are obligations that a company needs to settle within a year. They include:
    - Accounts payable: Money owed to suppliers for purchases made on credit.
    - Short-term debt: Loans or borrowings due within a year.
    - Accrued liabilities: Expenses that have been incurred but not yet paid.
    - Unearned revenue: Payments received in advance for services or goods to be delivered in the future.

Example of Working Capital Calculation

Let's consider a hypothetical company, ABC Corp, to illustrate how working capital is calculated. Assume the following financial data:

- Cash: $50,000
- Accounts receivable: $100,000
- Inventory: $150,000
- Accounts payable: $80,000
- Short-term debt: $50,000
- Accrued liabilities: $20,000

First, we calculate the total current assets:

Current Assets = $50,000 (Cash) + $100,000 (Accounts Receivable) + $150,000 (Inventory) = $300,000

Next, we calculate the total current liabilities:

Current Liabilities = $80,000 (Accounts Payable) + $50,000 (Short-term Debt) + $20,000 (Accrued Liabilities) = $150,000

Now, we can determine the working capital:

Working Capital = $300,000 (Current Assets) − $150,000 (Current Liabilities) = $150,000

ABC Corp has a positive working capital of $150,000, indicating it has sufficient short-term assets to cover its short-term liabilities.

Managing Working Capital

Effective management of working capital involves balancing the components to ensure liquidity without holding excessive assets that could otherwise be invested more productively. Here are some strategies for managing working capital:

1. **Inventory Management**: Optimize inventory levels to ensure that there is enough to meet demand without tying up too much capital. Techniques like Just-in-Time (JIT) inventory can help.

2. **Accounts Receivable**: Implement policies to expedite collections, such as offering early payment discounts, conducting credit checks on customers, and following up on overdue invoices promptly.

3. **Accounts Payable**: Manage payment terms with suppliers to take full advantage of any available discounts for early payments, but also consider stretching out payables to maintain liquidity.

4. **Cash Management**: Maintain an optimal level of cash reserves to meet unexpected needs while investing excess cash in short-term, liquid investments to earn returns.

5. **Short-term Financing**: Use short-term loans or lines of credit judiciously to manage temporary shortfalls, but avoid over-reliance on debt.

Working capital is a crucial indicator of a business's short-term financial health and operational efficiency. By understanding what working capital is and how to calculate it, business owners can better manage their resources, ensure liquidity, and support sustainable growth. Effective working capital management involves maintaining the right balance of current assets and liabilities, optimizing inventory levels, managing receivables and payables efficiently, and ensuring adequate cash reserves. By mastering these principles, businesses can enhance their financial stability and be better prepared to seize opportunities and navigate challenges.

Tips to Improve Working Capital 💡

1. **Increase Sales**: Boost your revenue by increasing sales or finding new customers.

2. **Manage Inventory**: Keep an optimal level of inventory – not too much, not too little.

3. **Negotiate Terms**: Try to extend payment terms with your suppliers and reduce terms with your customers.

4. **Reduce Expenses**: Cut unnecessary costs to improve your net income.

Understanding Liquidity Ratios: Key Indicators of Financial Health

Liquidity ratios are essential metrics used in financial analysis to evaluate a company's ability to meet its short-term obligations. These ratios provide insights into the financial stability of a business by measuring its capacity to convert assets into cash quickly. For investors, creditors, and managers, liquidity ratios are crucial in assessing the solvency and operational efficiency of a company. This section explores the concept of liquidity ratios, their importance, and the formulas used to calculate them.

What is a Liquidity Ratio?

Liquidity ratios are financial metrics that assess a company's ability to pay off its current liabilities with its current assets. These ratios are critical indicators of short-term financial health, as they reflect the company's capacity to generate enough cash to cover its immediate debts and obligations. The most commonly used liquidity ratios are:

1. **Current Ratio**: Measures the ability of a company to cover its short-term obligations with its current assets.

2. **Quick Ratio**: Also known as the acid-test ratio, it evaluates a company's capacity to pay off its current liabilities without relying on the sale of inventory.

3. **Cash Ratio**: This ratio is the most conservative measure of liquidity, considering only cash and cash equivalents in relation to current liabilities.

Importance of Liquidity Ratios

Liquidity ratios are vital for several reasons:

1. **Financial Health Assessment**: These ratios help in assessing the overall financial health and stability of a company, indicating whether it can meet its short-term obligations.

2. **Creditworthiness**: Creditors and lenders use liquidity ratios to determine a company's ability to repay loans and other debts, influencing their decision to extend credit.

3. **Operational Efficiency**: Liquidity ratios provide insights into how efficiently a company manages its assets and liabilities, reflecting its operational effectiveness.

4. **Investment Decisions**: Investors analyze liquidity ratios to gauge the risk associated with investing in a company. High liquidity ratios suggest lower risk, making the company a more attractive investment.

Calculating Liquidity Ratios

Let's delve into the formulas and interpretation of the three main liquidity ratios:

1. **Current Ratio**
2. **Quick Ratio**
3. **Cash Ratio**

Current Ratio

The current ratio measures a company's ability to pay off its short-term liabilities with its short-term assets. It is calculated using the following formula:

$$\text{Current Ratio} = \text{Current Assets} / \text{Current Liabilities}$$

- **Current Assets**: These include cash, accounts receivable, inventory, and other assets that are expected to be converted into cash within a year.
- **Current Liabilities**: These include accounts payable, short-term debt, and other obligations due within a year.

Example Current Ratio Calculation:

Suppose a company has current assets of $200,000 and current liabilities of $100,000. The current ratio would be:

Current Ratio = $200,000 / $100,000 = 2

A current ratio of 2 indicates that the company has twice as many current assets as it does current liabilities, suggesting a strong liquidity position.

Quick Ratio

The quick ratio, or acid-test ratio, provides a more stringent measure of liquidity by excluding inventory from current assets. The formula is:

$$\text{Quick Ratio} = \text{Current Assets} - \text{Inventory} / \text{Current Liabilities}$$

This ratio focuses on the most liquid assets that can be quickly converted into cash, such as cash, accounts receivable, and marketable securities.

Example Calculation:

If the company from the previous example has $50,000 in inventory, the quick ratio would be:

Quick Ratio = $200,000 − $50,000 / $100,000 = 1.5

A quick ratio of 1.5 means that the company has 1.5 times more liquid assets than its current liabilities, indicating a healthy liquidity position without relying on inventory sales.

Cash Ratio

The cash ratio is the most conservative liquidity ratio, considering only cash and cash equivalents. It is calculated using the following formula:

$$\text{Cash Ratio} = \frac{\text{Current Assets}}{\text{Current Liabilities}}$$

- **Cash and Cash Equivalents**: These include cash on hand and highly liquid investments that can be converted into cash within three months.

Example Calculation:

If the company has $80,000 in cash and cash equivalents, the cash ratio would be:

Cash Ratio = $80,000 / $100,000 = 0.8

A cash ratio of 0.8 indicates that the company has 80% of its current liabilities covered by cash and cash equivalents, suggesting a conservative approach to liquidity management.

Interpreting Liquidity Ratios

While calculating liquidity ratios is straightforward, interpreting them requires a deeper understanding of the company's context and industry standards:

1. **Industry Benchmarks**: Different industries have varying standards for liquidity ratios. For example, a current ratio of 1.5 might be acceptable in some industries but considered low in others.

2. **Trend Analysis**: Examining liquidity ratios over time helps identify trends and potential liquidity issues. A declining trend might signal financial distress, while an improving trend indicates enhanced liquidity.

3. **Comparison with Peers**: Comparing a company's liquidity ratios with those of its competitors provides insights into its relative financial health.

4. **Seasonality**: Some businesses experience seasonal fluctuations in liquidity. Understanding these patterns helps in interpreting the ratios accurately.

Managing Liquidity Ratios

Maintaining optimal liquidity ratios is crucial for a company's financial stability. Here are some strategies to manage liquidity effectively:

1. **Efficient Working Capital Management**: Optimize inventory levels, manage receivables and payables efficiently, and maintain an appropriate level of cash reserves.
2. **Cash Flow Forecasting**: Regularly forecast cash flows to anticipate and address potential liquidity shortfalls.
3. **Debt Management**: Balance short-term and long-term debt to ensure adequate liquidity without overburdening the company with debt obligations.
4. **Cost Control**: Monitor and control operational costs to preserve cash and maintain liquidity.

Liquidity ratios are vital tools for assessing a company's short-term financial health and operational efficiency. By measuring the ability to cover short-term obligations, these ratios provide crucial insights for investors, creditors, and managers. Understanding how to calculate and interpret liquidity ratios, such as the current ratio, quick ratio, and cash ratio, enables businesses to maintain financial stability, manage risks, and make informed decisions. Effective liquidity management ensures that a company can meet its immediate obligations, invest in growth opportunities, and sustain long-term success.

Understanding Current Ratio: A Key Indicator of Financial Health

The current ratio is a fundamental financial metric used to evaluate a company's ability to meet its short-term obligations with its short-term assets. It is a critical indicator of a company's liquidity and overall financial health. This section explains the concept of the current ratio, its significance, the formula to calculate it, and how to interpret and manage it effectively.

The current ratio, also known as the working capital ratio, is a liquidity ratio that measures a company's ability to pay off its short-term liabilities with its short-term assets. It provides insight into the efficiency of a company's operating cycle and its ability to turn its products into cash.

This formula expresses the current ratio as a numerical value, which represents how many times a company's current assets can cover its current liabilities.

Importance of the Current Ratio

The current ratio is crucial for several reasons:

1. **Liquidity Indicator**: It provides a direct measure of a company's liquidity, showing how well it can cover its short-term obligations.

2. **Operational Efficiency**: A higher current ratio indicates better operational efficiency and sound financial management.

3. **Creditworthiness**: Lenders and creditors use the current ratio to assess a company's creditworthiness and risk level. A higher ratio is often viewed more favorably.

4. **Financial Stability**: It helps in evaluating a company's short-term financial stability, ensuring that it has enough resources to continue its operations without financial strain.

5. **Investment Decision**: Investors use the current ratio to gauge a company's financial health and its ability to generate returns without liquidity issues.

Calculating the Current Ratio

To calculate the current ratio, you need to identify a company's current assets and current liabilities. The formula is:

$$\text{Current Ratio} = \text{Current Assets} / \text{Current Liabilities}$$

Here is a detailed breakdown of the components:

- **Current Assets**: These are assets that are expected to be converted into cash or used up within one year. They include cash and cash equivalents, accounts receivable, inventory, and other short-term assets.
- **Current Liabilities**: These are obligations that are due to be settled within one year. They include accounts payable, short-term loans, and other short-term debts.

Example Calculation

Let's consider a hypothetical company, ABC Corp, to illustrate how the current ratio is calculated. Assume the following financial data:

- Current Assets:
    - Cash: $50,000
    - Accounts Receivable: $30,000
    - Inventory: $20,000
    - Other Current Assets: $10,000
    - **Total Current Assets** = $110,000
- Current Liabilities:
    - Accounts Payable: $40,000
    - Short-term Loans: $30,000
    - Other Current Liabilities: $20,000
    - **Total Current Liabilities** = $90,000

Apply the current ratio formula:

Current Ratio = $110,000 / $90,000 = 1.22

A current ratio of 1.22 indicates that ABC Corp has $1.22 in current assets for every $1.00 of current liabilities.

Interpreting the Current Ratio

Interpreting the current ratio involves understanding its implications in the context of the company and its industry:

1. **Liquidity**: A current ratio greater than 1 indicates that the company has more current assets than current liabilities, which is generally positive and suggests good liquidity. A ratio less than 1 indicates potential liquidity problems.

2. **Industry Benchmarks**: Different industries have varying standards for acceptable current ratios. For example, industries with rapid inventory turnover may operate efficiently with lower current ratios, while others may require higher ratios to ensure liquidity.

3. **Trend Analysis**: Analyzing the current ratio over time helps identify trends in a company's liquidity. A rising ratio may indicate improving liquidity, while a declining ratio might signal potential liquidity issues.

4. **Comparison with Competitors**: Comparing a company's current ratio with those of its competitors provides insights into its relative liquidity and financial health.

Managing the Current Ratio

Maintaining an optimal current ratio is crucial for ensuring liquidity and financial stability. Here are some strategies to manage it effectively:

1. **Increase Current Assets**: Enhance liquidity by increasing cash reserves, improving accounts receivable collections, and managing inventory effectively.

2. **Reduce Current Liabilities**: Manage liabilities by negotiating longer payment terms with suppliers, refinancing short-term debt with long-term debt, and controlling operational expenses.

3. **Efficient Inventory Management**: Optimize inventory levels to avoid overstocking and reduce holding costs, while ensuring that enough inventory is available to meet demand.

4. **Improve Cash Flow Management**: Enhance cash flow by streamlining operations, reducing overhead costs, and implementing effective credit control measures.

5. **Financial Planning and Forecasting**: Regularly monitor and forecast cash flows to anticipate and address potential liquidity issues before they become critical.

Limitations of the Current Ratio

While the current ratio is a valuable measure of liquidity, it has its limitations:

1. **Does Not Reflect Cash Flow Timing**: The current ratio does not account for the timing of cash inflows and outflows, which can impact a company's actual liquidity.

2. **Varies by Industry**: The significance of the current ratio varies widely by industry, making it difficult to compare across different sectors.

3. **Potential for Misinterpretation**: A very high current ratio may indicate that a company is not utilizing its assets efficiently, while a very low ratio might signal liquidity issues or efficient use of resources.

4. **Ignores Quality of Assets**: The current ratio does not consider the quality of current assets. For example, inventory may include obsolete items that cannot be easily converted into cash.

The current ratio is a crucial financial metric that provides insights into a company's liquidity and ability to meet its short-term obligations. Calculating and interpreting the current ratio involves understanding the company's financial context and industry standards. A higher current ratio generally indicates better liquidity and financial stability, while a lower ratio suggests potential liquidity issues. Effective management of the current ratio through strategies such as increasing current assets, reducing current liabilities, efficient inventory management, improving cash flow management, and financial planning can ensure a company's financial health and long-term success. Despite its limitations, the current ratio remains an essential tool for assessing a company's liquidity and operational efficiency, helping investors, creditors, and managers make informed decisions.

Understanding the Quick Ratio: A Crucial Measure of Financial Liquidity

Financial liquidity is a key indicator of a company's ability to meet its short-term obligations, and one of the most precise measures of liquidity is the quick ratio, also known as the acid-test ratio. The quick ratio assesses a company's ability to pay off its current liabilities without relying on the sale of inventory, thus providing a more stringent evaluation of short-term financial health. This section details the quick ratio, explaining its importance, the formula to calculate it, and how to interpret and manage it effectively.

Importance of the Quick Ratio

The quick ratio is a financial metric that evaluates a company's ability to cover its short-term liabilities with its most liquid assets. Unlike the current ratio, which includes all current assets in its calculation, the quick ratio excludes inventory. This exclusion is significant because inventory is not as readily convertible to cash as other current assets, such as cash and accounts receivable. Therefore, the quick ratio offers a more conservative view of a company's liquidity position.

Calculating the Quick Ratio

To calculate the quick ratio, you need to identify a company's current assets, inventory, and current liabilities. The quick ratio, or acid-test ratio, provides a more stringent measure of liquidity by excluding inventory from current assets. The formula is:

Quick Ratio = (Current Assets minus Inventory) / (Current Liabilities)

Here is a detailed breakdown of the components:

- **Current Assets**: These are assets that are expected to be converted into cash within a year. They include cash, accounts receivable, and marketable securities.

- **Inventory**: This consists of goods available for sale. Since inventory is not as liquid as other current assets, it is excluded from the quick ratio.

- **Current Liabilities**: These are obligations the company must settle within a year, such as accounts payable, short-term debt, and other similar liabilities.

This ratio focuses on the most liquid assets that can be quickly converted into cash, such as cash, accounts receivable, and marketable securities.

Example Calculation:

If the company from the previous example has $50,000 in inventory, the quick ratio would be:

Quick Ratio = $200,000 − $50,000 / $100,000 = 1.5

A quick ratio of 1.5 means that the company has 1.5 times more liquid assets than its current liabilities, indicating a healthy liquidity position without relying on inventory sales.

This formula highlights the company's liquid assets—those that can quickly be turned into cash—against its short-term obligations.

Importance of the Quick Ratio

The quick ratio is crucial for several reasons:

1. **Liquidity Assessment**: It provides a clear picture of a company's immediate liquidity, excluding assets that might take time to liquidate.

2. **Creditworthiness**: Lenders and creditors often look at the quick ratio to evaluate a company's ability to repay short-term debts without relying on the sale of inventory.

3. **Financial Health Indicator**: A strong quick ratio indicates robust financial health, as it shows the company can cover its liabilities with its most liquid assets.

4. **Risk Management**: By focusing on the most liquid assets, the quick ratio helps in assessing the company's risk of insolvency.

Example Calculation

Let's consider a hypothetical company, XYZ Corp, to illustrate how the quick ratio is calculated. Assume the following financial data:

- Cash: $40,000
- Accounts receivable: $60,000
- Inventory: $50,000
- Accounts payable: $30,000
- Short-term debt: $20,000

First, calculate the total current assets:

Current Assets = $40,000 (Cash) + $60,000 (Accounts Receivable) = $100,000

Next, determine the current liabilities:

Current Liabilities = $30,000 (Accounts Payable) + $20,000 (Short-term Debt) = $50,000

Now, apply the quick ratio formula:

Quick Ratio = $100,000 (Current Assets) − $50,000 (Inventory) / $50,000 (Current Liabilities) = $50,000 = 1

A quick ratio of 1 indicates that XYZ Corp has exactly enough liquid assets to cover its current liabilities, without relying on inventory sales.

Interpreting the Quick Ratio

Interpreting the quick ratio involves understanding the context of the company and its industry:

1. **Benchmarking**: Different industries have varying standards for an acceptable quick ratio. Generally, a ratio above 1 is considered good, as it indicates that the company can cover its short-term liabilities without selling inventory.

2. **Trend Analysis**: Analyzing the quick ratio over time helps in identifying trends in a company's liquidity. A declining ratio might indicate worsening liquidity, while an increasing ratio suggests improved financial health.

3. **Comparison with Peers**: Comparing a company's quick ratio with those of its competitors provides insights into its relative liquidity position.

4. **Seasonal Variations**: Some businesses experience seasonal fluctuations in liquidity. Understanding these patterns is essential for accurately interpreting the quick ratio.

Managing the Quick Ratio

Maintaining an optimal quick ratio is crucial for ensuring financial stability. Here are some strategies to manage it effectively:

1. **Efficient Receivables Management**: Implement policies to expedite collections, such as offering early payment discounts and conducting regular follow-ups on overdue accounts.

2. **Cash Management**: Maintain adequate cash reserves to cover short-term liabilities. This involves prudent cash flow management and investing in short-term, liquid assets.

3. **Controlling Expenses**: Monitor and control operational costs to preserve cash and improve liquidity.

4. **Short-term Financing**: Use short-term loans judiciously to manage temporary liquidity shortfalls, but avoid over-reliance on debt.

5. **Inventory Management**: While inventory is excluded from the quick ratio, managing it efficiently ensures that other liquidity measures remain strong. Techniques like Just-in-Time (JIT) inventory can help in minimizing excess stock.

Limitations of the Quick Ratio

While the quick ratio is a valuable measure of liquidity, it has its limitations:

1. **Exclusion of Inventory**: By excluding inventory, the quick ratio may not fully represent the liquidity of companies with highly liquid inventory.

2. **Static Measure**: The quick ratio provides a snapshot of liquidity at a specific point in time and may not reflect future liquidity positions.

3. **Does Not Consider Cash Flow**: The quick ratio does not account for the timing of cash flows, which can impact a company's ability to meet its short-term obligations.

The quick ratio is a critical financial metric that offers a stringent measure of a company's liquidity by focusing on its most liquid assets. By excluding inventory, the quick ratio provides a conservative assessment of a company's ability to meet its short-term obligations. Calculating and interpreting the quick ratio involves understanding the company's financial context and industry standards. Effective management of the quick ratio through efficient receivables management, cash management, expense control, and prudent use of short-term financing can ensure a company's financial stability and operational efficiency. Despite its limitations, the quick ratio remains an essential tool for assessing the short-term financial health of a business.

Understanding the Cash Ratio: A Critical Measure of Liquidity

The cash ratio is a stringent financial metric used to assess a company's ability to pay off its short-term liabilities using its most liquid assets—cash and cash equivalents. This section delves into the concept of the cash ratio, its significance, the formula to calculate it, and how to interpret and manage it effectively.

What is the Cash Ratio?

The cash ratio is a conservative liquidity ratio that measures a company's ability to cover its short-term obligations with its cash and cash equivalents alone. Unlike other liquidity ratios such as the current ratio and quick ratio, the cash ratio excludes inventory and receivables from its calculation, focusing solely on the most liquid assets.

This formula expresses the cash ratio as a numerical value, which represents how many times a company's cash and cash equivalents can cover its current liabilities.

Importance of the Cash Ratio

The cash ratio is crucial for several reasons:

1. **Stringent Liquidity Measure**: It provides the most conservative view of a company's liquidity, highlighting its ability to meet short-term obligations without relying on the sale of inventory or collection of receivables.

2. **Risk Assessment**: It helps in assessing the financial risk associated with a company. A higher cash ratio indicates lower liquidity risk.

3. **Creditworthiness**: Lenders and creditors often look at the cash ratio to evaluate a company's ability to repay short-term debts, especially during financial distress.

4. **Financial Stability**: It serves as an indicator of financial stability and cash management practices, ensuring that the company can withstand unexpected financial shocks.

5. **Investor Confidence**: A strong cash ratio can enhance investor confidence by demonstrating the company's robust cash position and prudent financial management.

Calculating the Cash Ratio

To calculate the cash ratio, you need to identify a company's cash and cash equivalents and its current liabilities. The formula is:

Cash Ratio = Cash and Cash Equivalents / Current Liabilities

Here is a detailed breakdown of the components:

- **Cash and Cash Equivalents**: These are the most liquid assets on a company's balance sheet. They include physical cash, bank balances, and short-term investments that are easily convertible to cash.
- **Current Liabilities**: These are obligations that are due to be settled within one year. They include accounts payable, short-term loans, and other short-term debts.

Example Calculation

Let's consider a hypothetical company, XYZ Corp, to illustrate how the cash ratio is calculated. Assume the following financial data:

- Cash and Cash Equivalents: $50,000
- Current Liabilities:
    - Accounts Payable: $30,000
    - Short-term Loans: $20,000
    - Other Current Liabilities: $10,000
    - **Total Current Liabilities** = $60,000

Apply the cash ratio formula:

Cash Ratio = $50,000 / $60,000 = 0.83

A cash ratio of 0.83 indicates that XYZ Corp has $0.83 in cash and cash equivalents for every $1.00 of current liabilities.

Interpreting the Cash Ratio

Interpreting the cash ratio involves understanding its implications in the context of the company and its industry:

1. **Liquidity**: A cash ratio of less than 1 indicates that the company does not have enough cash to cover its short-term liabilities fully, suggesting potential liquidity concerns. A ratio greater than 1 indicates strong liquidity.
2. **Industry Benchmarks**: Different industries have varying standards for acceptable cash ratios. Industries with stable cash flows may operate efficiently with lower cash ratios, while more volatile industries may require higher ratios to ensure liquidity.

3. **Trend Analysis**: Analyzing the cash ratio over time helps identify trends in a company's liquidity and cash management practices. A rising ratio may indicate improved liquidity, while a declining ratio might signal potential cash flow issues.

4. **Comparison with Competitors**: Comparing a company's cash ratio with those of its competitors provides insights into its relative liquidity and financial health.

Managing the Cash Ratio

Maintaining an optimal cash ratio is crucial for ensuring liquidity and financial stability. Here are some strategies to manage it effectively:

1. **Improve Cash Reserves**: Enhance liquidity by increasing cash reserves through effective cash flow management, cost control, and prudent financial planning.

2. **Efficient Cash Management**: Implement efficient cash management practices to optimize the use of cash and cash equivalents, including timely collection of receivables and strategic timing of payments.

3. **Reduce Current Liabilities**: Manage liabilities by negotiating longer payment terms with suppliers, refinancing short-term debt with long-term debt, and controlling operational expenses.

4. **Short-term Investments**: Maintain a portfolio of short-term investments that can be quickly converted into cash without significant loss of value.

5. **Emergency Funds**: Establish emergency funds or credit lines to ensure the availability of cash during unexpected financial difficulties.

Limitations of the Cash Ratio

While the cash ratio is a valuable measure of liquidity, it has its limitations:

1. **Overly Conservative**: The cash ratio is very conservative and may not reflect the true liquidity position of companies that efficiently manage their receivables and inventories.

2. **Ignores Non-Cash Assets**: It excludes receivables and inventory, which can also be quickly converted into cash in normal operating conditions.

3. **Varies by Industry**: The significance of the cash ratio varies widely by industry, making it difficult to compare across different sectors.

4. **Potential Misinterpretation**: A very high cash ratio might indicate that the company is not using its cash effectively to invest in growth opportunities, while a very low ratio could signal liquidity issues.

The cash ratio is a crucial financial metric that provides insights into a company's ability to meet its short-term obligations using its most liquid assets. Calculating and interpreting the cash ratio involves understanding the company's financial context and industry standards. A higher cash ratio generally indicates better liquidity and financial stability, while a lower ratio suggests potential liquidity issues. Effective management of the cash ratio through strategies such as improving cash reserves, efficient cash management, reducing current liabilities, maintaining short-term investments, and establishing emergency funds can ensure a company's financial health and long-term success. Despite its limitations, the cash ratio remains an essential tool for assessing a company's liquidity and cash management practices, helping investors, creditors, and managers make informed decisions.

Understanding the Debt Ratio: Measuring Financial Leverage and Risk

The debt ratio is a critical financial metric used to assess a company's financial leverage and risk by measuring the proportion of its assets that are financed through debt. This ratio provides insights into a company's capital structure, financial stability, and ability to meet its long-term obligations. This section will help you understand the concept of the debt ratio, its significance, the formula to calculate it, and how to interpret and manage it effectively.

What is the Debt Ratio?

The debt ratio is a financial metric that indicates the percentage of a company's assets that are financed by debt. It is used to evaluate the level of financial leverage a company is using and to assess the risk associated with its capital structure. A higher debt ratio suggests that a larger portion of the company's assets is financed by debt, which can indicate higher financial risk. Conversely, a lower debt ratio suggests a more conservative financing approach, with a greater reliance on equity.

Definition: Debt Ratio = Total Debt / Total Assets

This formula highlights the proportion of a company's assets that are financed through debt, providing a snapshot of its financial leverage.

Importance of the Debt Ratio

The debt ratio is crucial for several reasons:

1. **Risk Assessment**: It helps in assessing the financial risk associated with a company's capital structure. A higher debt ratio indicates greater financial risk, as the company relies more on borrowed funds.

2. **Creditworthiness**: Lenders and investors use the debt ratio to evaluate a company's ability to meet its debt obligations. A lower debt ratio suggests a stronger financial position and higher creditworthiness.

3. **Financial Stability**: The debt ratio provides insights into a company's financial stability. A balanced ratio indicates prudent financial management, ensuring the company can sustain its operations and growth.

4. **Investment Decisions**: Investors analyze the debt ratio to gauge the level of financial leverage and risk involved in investing in a company. A lower debt ratio may indicate a safer investment.

Calculating the Debt Ratio

To calculate the debt ratio, you need to identify a company's total debt and total assets. The formula is:

Debt Ratio=Total Debt /Total Assets

Here is a detailed breakdown of the components:

- **Total Debt**: This includes both short-term debt (such as accounts payable and short-term loans) and long-term debt (such as bonds and long-term loans).

- **Total Assets**: These include current assets (such as cash, accounts receivable, and inventory) and non-current assets (such as property, plant, and equipment).

Example Calculation

Let's consider a hypothetical company, ABC Corp, to illustrate how the debt ratio is calculated. Assume the following financial data:

- Short-term debt: $100,000
- Long-term debt: $300,000
- Total assets: $1,000,000

First, calculate the total debt:

Total Debt = $100,000 (Short-term Debt) + $300,000 (Long-term Debt) = $400,000

Next, apply the debt ratio formula:

Debt Ratio = $400,000 (Total Debt) / $1,000,000 (Total Assets) = 0.4

A debt ratio of 0.4, or 40%, indicates that 40% of ABC Corp's assets are financed through debt, suggesting a moderate level of financial leverage.

Interpreting the Debt Ratio

Interpreting the debt ratio involves understanding the context of the company and its industry:

1. **Industry Benchmarks**: Different industries have varying standards for acceptable debt ratios. For example, capital-intensive industries like utilities may have higher debt ratios, while technology companies may have lower debt ratios.

2. **Trend Analysis**: Analyzing the debt ratio over time helps identify trends in a company's financial leverage. A rising ratio may indicate increasing financial risk, while a declining ratio suggests improved financial stability.

3. **Comparison with Peers**: Comparing a company's debt ratio with those of its competitors provides insights into its relative financial leverage and risk.

4. **Economic Conditions**: Economic conditions can impact the ideal debt ratio. During economic downturns, companies with lower debt ratios are typically better positioned to weather financial challenges.

Managing the Debt Ratio

Maintaining an optimal debt ratio is crucial for ensuring financial stability and minimizing risk. Here are some strategies to manage it effectively:

1. **Debt Management**: Carefully manage both short-term and long-term debt to maintain a balanced capital structure. Avoid excessive reliance on debt financing, which can increase financial risk.

2. **Equity Financing**: Consider raising funds through equity financing to reduce the debt ratio and improve financial stability. Issuing new shares or retaining earnings are common methods of equity financing.

3. **Revenue Growth**: Focus on revenue growth to increase total assets without proportionally increasing debt. This can help in reducing the debt ratio.

4. **Cost Control**: Monitor and control operational costs to improve profitability and free up cash for debt repayment. This can help in reducing the debt ratio over time.

5. **Cash Flow Management**: Efficient cash flow management ensures that the company can meet its debt obligations without straining its resources.

Limitations of the Debt Ratio

While the debt ratio is a valuable measure of financial leverage, it has its limitations:

1. **Does Not Consider Interest Rates**: The debt ratio does not account for the interest rates on debt, which can impact a company's ability to service its debt.

2. **Does Not Reflect Cash Flow**: The ratio does not consider the company's cash flow, which is crucial for meeting debt obligations.

3. **Static Measure**: The debt ratio provides a snapshot of financial leverage at a specific point in time and may not reflect future financial positions.

The debt ratio is a critical financial metric that provides insights into a company's financial leverage and risk by measuring the proportion of assets financed through debt. Calculating and interpreting the debt ratio involves understanding the company's financial context and industry standards. A balanced debt ratio indicates prudent financial management, ensuring the company can sustain its operations and growth. Effective management of the debt ratio through careful debt management, equity financing, revenue growth, cost control, and efficient cash flow management can ensure a company's financial stability and minimize risk. Despite its limitations, the debt ratio remains an essential tool for assessing the long-term financial health of a business.

Understanding Gross Margin: A Key Indicator of Business Profitability

Gross margin is a fundamental financial metric that provides insight into a company's profitability by measuring the difference between revenue and the cost of goods sold (COGS). It is crucial for understanding how efficiently a company is producing and selling its products. This section conveys the concept of gross margin, its significance, the formula to calculate it, and how to interpret and manage it effectively.

What is Gross Margin?

Gross margin, also known as **gross profit margin**, represents the percentage of revenue that exceeds the cost of goods sold. It indicates how well a company manages its production costs relative to its revenue. A higher gross margin means the company retains more money from each dollar of sales to cover other expenses and generate profit.

This formula expresses gross margin as a percentage, highlighting the portion of sales revenue that exceeds the direct costs of producing the goods or services sold.

Importance of Gross Margin

Gross margin is crucial for several reasons:

1. **Profitability Indicator**: It provides a direct measure of a company's profitability at the production level, indicating how efficiently it turns revenue into gross profit.

2. **Cost Management**: By analyzing gross margin, businesses can identify areas where they can reduce production costs or increase pricing to improve profitability.

3. **Pricing Strategy**: Understanding gross margin helps in setting appropriate pricing strategies that ensure competitiveness while maintaining profitability.

4. **Financial Health**: Investors and creditors use gross margin to assess a company's financial health and operational efficiency. A stable or increasing gross margin is a positive sign.

5. **Benchmarking**: Companies use gross margin to compare their performance against industry benchmarks and competitors, helping them understand their market position.

Calculating Gross Margin

To calculate gross margin, you need to identify a company's revenue and cost of goods sold (COGS). The formula is:

Gross Margin = Revenue − COGS × 100

Here is a detailed breakdown of the components:

- **Revenue**: This is the total amount of money generated from the sale of goods or services before any expenses are deducted.
- **Cost of Goods Sold (COGS)**: This includes all direct costs associated with producing the goods or services sold by the company, such as raw materials, labor, and manufacturing overhead.

Example Calculation

Let's consider a hypothetical company, XYZ Corp, to illustrate how gross margin is calculated. Assume the following financial data:

- Revenue: $500,000
- Cost of Goods Sold (COGS): $300,000

First, calculate the gross profit:

Gross Profit = Revenue − COGS = $500,000 − $300,000 = $200,000

Next, apply the gross margin formula:

Gross Margin = $200,000 / $500,000 × 100 = 40%

A gross margin of 40% indicates that XYZ Corp retains 40 cents from each dollar of sales after covering the direct costs of production.

Interpreting Gross Margin

Interpreting gross margin involves understanding the context of the company and its industry:

1. **Industry Benchmarks**: Different industries have varying standards for acceptable gross margins. For example, software companies typically have higher gross margins compared to manufacturing companies due to lower production costs.
2. **Trend Analysis**: Analyzing gross margin over time helps identify trends in a company's profitability. A rising margin may indicate improved cost management or successful pricing strategies, while a declining margin might signal increasing production costs or pricing pressures.

3. **Comparison with Competitors**: Comparing a company's gross margin with those of its competitors provides insights into its relative operational efficiency and market position.

4. **Impact of Economic Conditions**: Economic conditions can affect gross margin. For instance, during economic downturns, companies may face increased pricing pressures, leading to lower gross margins.

Managing Gross Margin

Maintaining an optimal gross margin is crucial for ensuring profitability and financial stability. Here are some strategies to manage it effectively:

1. **Cost Control**: Implement cost control measures to reduce COGS. This can include negotiating better terms with suppliers, improving production processes, and reducing waste.

2. **Pricing Strategy**: Adjust pricing strategies to ensure they reflect the value provided to customers while maintaining competitiveness. This may involve premium pricing for high-quality products or competitive pricing for cost-sensitive markets.

3. **Product Mix**: Optimize the product mix to focus on high-margin products. Analyzing the profitability of different products can help in prioritizing those with higher margins.

4. **Operational Efficiency**: Improve operational efficiency by investing in technology and automation. Streamlining production processes can lead to cost savings and higher gross margins.

5. **Market Expansion**: Expand into new markets or customer segments to increase sales revenue without significantly increasing COGS. This can help in improving gross margin through higher sales volumes.

Limitations of Gross Margin

While gross margin is a valuable measure of profitability, it has its limitations:

1. **Does Not Reflect Overall Profitability**: Gross margin only considers direct production costs and does not account for other operating expenses such as marketing, administration, and interest.

2. **Varies by Industry**: The significance of gross margin varies widely by industry, making it difficult to compare across different sectors.

3. **Can Be Manipulated**: Companies might manipulate gross margin by changing accounting practices related to COGS, such as inventory valuation methods.

Gross margin is a crucial financial metric that provides insights into a company's profitability by measuring the difference between revenue and the cost of goods sold. Calculating and interpreting gross margin involves understanding the company's financial context and industry standards. A high gross margin indicates efficient cost management and strong profitability, while a low margin suggests potential issues with production costs or pricing strategies. Effective management of gross margin through cost control, pricing strategies, product mix optimization, operational efficiency, and market expansion can ensure a company's financial stability and long-term success. Despite its limitations, gross margin remains an essential tool for assessing the operational efficiency and profitability of a business.

Understanding Profit Margin: A Comprehensive Indicator of Business Success

Profit margin is a fundamental financial metric that measures the extent to which a company or a business activity generates profit from its sales. It indicates the efficiency of a company in controlling its costs and pricing its products or services to generate earnings. This section uncovers the concept of profit margin, its significance, the formula to calculate it, and how to interpret and manage it effectively.

What is Profit Margin?

Profit margin, also known as **net profit margin**, represents the percentage of revenue that remains as profit after all expenses are deducted. It provides insight into a company's overall profitability by showing how much profit is made for every dollar of revenue generated.

This formula expresses profit margin as a percentage, highlighting the portion of revenue that is retained as profit after covering all costs and expenses.

Importance of Profit Margin

Profit margin is crucial for several reasons:

1. **Profitability Indicator**: It provides a direct measure of a company's profitability, showing how efficiently it converts revenue into profit.

2. **Cost Management**: By analyzing profit margin, businesses can identify areas where they can reduce costs or increase efficiency to improve profitability.

3. **Pricing Strategy**: Understanding profit margin helps in setting appropriate pricing strategies that ensure competitiveness while maintaining profitability.

4. **Financial Health**: Investors and creditors use profit margin to assess a company's financial health and operational efficiency. A stable or increasing profit margin is a positive sign.

5. **Benchmarking**: Companies use profit margin to compare their performance against industry benchmarks and competitors, helping them understand their market position.

Calculating Profit Margin

To calculate profit margin, you need to identify a company's net profit and revenue. The formula is:

Profit Margin = Net Profit / Revenue × 100

Here is a detailed breakdown of the components:

- **Revenue**: This is the total amount of money generated from the sale of goods or services before any expenses are deducted.
- **Net Profit**: This is the profit remaining after all expenses, including cost of goods sold (COGS), operating expenses, interest, taxes, and other costs, have been deducted from revenue.

Example Calculation

Let's consider a hypothetical company, XYZ Corp, to illustrate how profit margin is calculated. Assume the following financial data:

- Revenue: $1,000,000
- Net Profit: $150,000

Apply the profit margin formula:

Profit Margin = $150,000 / $1,000,000 × 100 = 15%

A profit margin of 15% indicates that XYZ Corp retains 15 cents from each dollar of sales as profit after covering all expenses.

Interpreting Profit Margin

Interpreting profit margin involves understanding the context of the company and its industry:

1. **Industry Benchmarks**: Different industries have varying standards for acceptable profit margins. For example, software companies typically have higher profit margins compared to retail businesses due to lower operating costs.
2. **Trend Analysis**: Analyzing profit margin over time helps identify trends in a company's profitability. A rising margin may indicate improved cost management or successful pricing strategies, while a declining margin might signal increasing costs or pricing pressures.
3. **Comparison with Competitors**: Comparing a company's profit margin with those of its competitors provides insights into its relative operational efficiency and market position.
4. **Impact of Economic Conditions**: Economic conditions can affect profit margin. For instance, during economic downturns, companies may face increased pricing pressures, leading to lower profit margins.

Managing Profit Margin

Maintaining an optimal profit margin is crucial for ensuring profitability and financial stability. Here are some strategies to manage it effectively:

1. **Cost Control**: Implement cost control measures to reduce operating expenses. This can include negotiating better terms with suppliers, improving production processes, and reducing waste.

2. **Pricing Strategy**: Adjust pricing strategies to ensure they reflect the value provided to customers while maintaining competitiveness. This may involve premium pricing for high-quality products or competitive pricing for cost-sensitive markets.

3. **Product Mix**: Optimize the product mix to focus on high-margin products. Analyzing the profitability of different products can help in prioritizing those with higher margins.

4. **Operational Efficiency**: Improve operational efficiency by investing in technology and automation. Streamlining production processes can lead to cost savings and higher profit margins.

5. **Market Expansion**: Expand into new markets or customer segments to increase sales revenue without significantly increasing operating expenses. This can help in improving profit margin through higher sales volumes.

Limitations of Profit Margin

While profit margin is a valuable measure of profitability, it has its limitations:

1. **Does Not Reflect Cash Flow**: Profit margin does not account for the timing of cash flows, which can impact a company's ability to meet its financial obligations.

2. **Varies by Industry**: The significance of profit margin varies widely by industry, making it difficult to compare across different sectors.

3. **Can Be Manipulated**: Companies might manipulate profit margin by changing accounting practices related to revenue recognition and expense allocation.

Profit margin is a crucial financial metric that provides insights into a company's profitability by measuring the difference between revenue and net profit. Calculating and interpreting profit margin involves understanding the company's financial context and industry standards. A high profit margin indicates efficient cost management and strong profitability, while a low margin suggests potential issues with operating expenses or pricing strategies. Effective management of profit margin through cost control, pricing strategies, product mix optimization, operational efficiency, and market expansion can ensure a company's financial stability and long-term success. Despite its limitations, profit margin remains an essential tool for assessing the operational efficiency and profitability of a business.

Understanding Return on Equity (ROE): A Key Indicator of Shareholder Value

Return on Equity (ROE) is a fundamental financial metric used to assess a company's ability to generate profits from its shareholders' equity. It provides insights into how effectively a company is using the funds invested by its shareholders to generate earnings. This section unlocks the concept of ROE, its significance, the formula to calculate it, and how to interpret and manage it effectively.

What is Return on Equity?

Return on Equity (ROE) is a measure of a company's profitability in relation to shareholders' equity. It indicates how much profit a company generates with the money shareholders have invested. A higher ROE signifies that the company is more efficient at converting the equity financing it receives into profits.

This formula expresses ROE as a percentage, highlighting the return generated on every dollar of shareholders' equity.

Importance of Return on Equity

ROE is crucial for several reasons:

1. **Profitability Indicator**: It provides a direct measure of how efficiently a company is generating profits from its shareholders' equity.

2. **Management Efficiency**: ROE reflects the effectiveness of a company's management in utilizing equity capital to generate earnings.

3. **Investment Attractiveness**: Investors use ROE to assess the attractiveness of investing in a company. A higher ROE generally indicates a potentially more profitable investment.

4. **Benchmarking**: Companies use ROE to compare their performance against industry benchmarks and competitors, helping them understand their market position.

5. **Shareholder Value**: ROE is a key indicator of the value being created for shareholders, aligning with their interests in maximizing returns on their investments.

Calculating Return on Equity

To calculate ROE, you need to identify a company's net income and shareholders' equity. The formula is:

ROE= (Profit or Loss) / Equity × 100

Here is a detailed breakdown of the components:

- **Net Income**: This is the total profit of a company after all expenses, taxes, and interest have been deducted from total revenue.
- **Shareholders' Equity**: This is the amount of equity financing provided by shareholders, calculated as total assets minus total liabilities.

Example Calculation

Let's consider a hypothetical company, ABC Corp, to illustrate how ROE is calculated. Assume the following financial data:

- Net Income: $200,000
- Shareholders' Equity: $1,000,000

Apply the ROE formula:

ROE = $200,000 / $1,000,000 × 100 = 20%

An ROE of 20% indicates that ABC Corp generates a profit of 20 cents for every dollar of shareholders' equity.

Interpreting Return on Equity

Interpreting ROE involves understanding the context of the company and its industry:

1. **Industry Benchmarks**: Different industries have varying standards for acceptable ROE. For example, technology companies often have higher ROEs compared to utilities due to different capital structures and profit margins.
2. **Trend Analysis**: Analyzing ROE over time helps identify trends in a company's profitability and management efficiency. A rising ROE may indicate improving financial performance, while a declining ROE might signal potential issues.
3. **Comparison with Competitors**: Comparing a company's ROE with those of its competitors provides insights into its relative performance and market position.

4. **Impact of Financial Leverage**: Companies with high financial leverage (i.e., high levels of debt) might show a high ROE due to the smaller equity base, but this also indicates higher financial risk.

Managing Return on Equity

Maintaining an optimal ROE is crucial for ensuring profitability and shareholder value. Here are some strategies to manage it effectively:

1. **Revenue Growth**: Focus on increasing revenue through market expansion, product development, and improved sales strategies to boost net income.

2. **Cost Control**: Implement cost control measures to reduce operating expenses, which can lead to higher net income and improved ROE.

3. **Efficient Use of Assets**: Enhance the efficient use of assets to generate higher returns. This can include optimizing inventory levels and improving asset utilization.

4. **Debt Management**: Carefully manage the use of debt to leverage returns without significantly increasing financial risk. Properly balancing debt and equity can enhance ROE.

5. **Dividend Policy**: Maintain a dividend policy that balances rewarding shareholders with retaining earnings for reinvestment in growth opportunities.

Limitations of Return on Equity

While ROE is a valuable measure of profitability, it has its limitations:

1. **Impact of Leverage**: High financial leverage can inflate ROE, making it appear more attractive than it truly is. It's essential to consider the debt levels when evaluating ROE.

2. **Does Not Reflect Cash Flow**: ROE does not account for the timing of cash flows, which can impact a company's ability to meet its financial obligations.

3. **Varies by Industry**: The significance of ROE varies widely by industry, making it difficult to compare across different sectors.

4. **Potential for Manipulation**: Companies might manipulate ROE by changing accounting practices related to revenue recognition and expense allocation.

Return on Equity (ROE) is a crucial financial metric that provides insights into a company's profitability and management efficiency by measuring the return generated on shareholders' equity. Calculating and interpreting ROE involves understanding the company's financial context and industry standards. A high ROE indicates efficient use of equity capital and strong profitability, while a low ROE suggests potential issues with generating earnings from shareholders' investments. Effective management of ROE through revenue growth, cost control, efficient use of assets, debt management, and balanced dividend policies can ensure a company's financial stability and long-term success. Despite its limitations, ROE remains an essential tool for assessing the operational efficiency and profitability of a business, helping investors and stakeholders make informed decisions.

WORKSHEETS

INCOME STATEMENT RATIOS

Gross Profit Margin
Profit Margin
Return on Equity (ROE)

INCOME STATEMENT

Sunny's Sweets Bakery Income Statement Fiscal Year-Ending December 31, 2023		
Revenue		**Amount ($)**
Sales Revenue		150,000
Other Income		5,000
Total Revenue		**155,000**
Cost of Goods Sold (COGS)		
Ingredients		30,000
Packaging		5,000
Direct Labor		20,000
Total COGS		**55,000**
Gross Profit	(Total Revenue - Total COGS)	**100,000**
Operating Expenses		
Rent		15,000
Utilities		5,000
Salaries and Wages		25,000
Advertising		10,000
Supplies		3,000
Insurance		2,000
Depreciation		4,000
Miscellaneous Expenses		1,000
Total Operating Expenses		**65,000**
Operating Income	(Gross Profit - Total Operating Expenses)	**35,000**
Other Expenses		
Interest Expense		2,000
Total Other Expenses		2,000
Net Profit	(Operating Income - Other Expenses)	**33,000**

INCOME STATEMENT BREAKDOWN

Total Revenue: $150,000 (Sales Revenue) + $5,000 (Other Income) = $155,000

Total COGS: $30,000 (Ingredients) + $5,000 (Packaging) + $20,000 (Direct Labor) = $55,000

Gross Profit: $155,000 (Total Revenue) – $55,000 (Total COGS) = $100,000\$155,000

Total Operating Expenses: $15,000 (Rent) + $5,000 (Utilities) + $25,000 (Salaries and Wages) + $10,000 (Advertising) +$ 3,000 (Supplies) + $2,000 (Insurance) + $4,000 (Depreciation) + $1,000 (Miscellaneous Expenses) = $65,000

Operating Income: $100,000 (Gross Profit) – $65,000 (Total Operating Expenses) = $35,000

Total Other Expenses: $2,000 (Interest Expense) = $2,000

Net Profit: $35,000 (Operating Income) – $2,000 (Total Other Expenses) = $33,000

FIRST-QUARTER

Gross Profit Margin
Profit Margin
Return on Equity (ROE)

GROSS PROFIT MARGIN

GROSS MARGIN REPRESENTS THE PERCENTAGE OF REVENUE THAT EXCEEDS THE COST OF GOODS SOLD. IT INDICATES HOW WELL A COMPANY MANAGES ITS PRODUCTION COSTS RELATIVE TO ITS REVENUE.

STEP 1 You need two items from **Income Statement**

Revenue generated from product sold — TOTAL REVENUE $

Use **all direct costs** for producing goods — TOTAL COGS $

STEP 2 Use the magic formula

Gross Margin = (Revenue − COGS) $

Divide by Revenue $

Multiply by 100 $

Gross Margin = %

Tips to Improve Gross Margin

- Increase Sales Prices: Consider adjusting your prices to better reflect the value of your products.

- Reduce Production Costs: Look for ways to cut costs in production, such as negotiating better prices for materials or improving production efficiency.

- Optimize Inventory: Manage your inventory effectively to reduce waste and ensure you're not overstocking or understocking.

PROFIT MARGIN

PROFIT MARGIN, ALSO KNOWN AS **NET PROFIT MARGIN**, REPRESENTS THE PERCENTAGE OF REVENUE THAT REMAINS AS PROFIT AFTER ALL EXPENSES ARE DEDUCTED.

STEP 1 You need two items from **Income Statement**

Net Profit minus all expenses from total revenue	NET PROFIT	$
This all monies made from sales	REVENUE	$

STEP 2 Use the magic formula

Net Profit	$
Divided by Revenue	$
Multiply by 100	$
Profit Margin =	%

STEP 3 Interpret Results

High Profit Margin
🎉 Awesome! You're making a good profit from your sales.

Low Profit Margin
😟 Don't worry! You might need to find ways to reduce costs or increase sales prices.

RETURN ON EQUITY

RETURN ON EQUITY (ROE) IS A MEASURE OF A COMPANY'S PROFITABILITY IN RELATION TO SHAREHOLDERS' EQUITY.

STEP 1 You need two items from **Income Statement**

Total profit after all expenses	NET INCOME	$
All **shareholder's** hold in the company	EQUITY	$

STEP 2 Use the magic formula

Net Income = (Total Income - Total Expenses)	$
Divide by Shareholder's Equity	$
Multiply by 100	$
Return on Equity (ROE)	%

Tips to Improve Return on Equity

- Increase Net Income: Boost profitability through increased sales, cost reduction, and improving operational efficiency.

- Efficient Use of Equity: Ensure that investments and retained earnings are being used effectively to generate profit.

- Strategic Financial Decisions: Make informed decisions about reinvesting profits, paying dividends, or raising additional equity to maximize returns.

SECOND-QUARTER

Gross Profit Margin
Profit Margin
Return on Equity (ROE)

GROSS PROFIT MARGIN

GROSS MARGIN REPRESENTS THE PERCENTAGE OF REVENUE THAT EXCEEDS THE COST OF GOODS SOLD. IT INDICATES HOW WELL A COMPANY MANAGES ITS PRODUCTION COSTS RELATIVE TO ITS REVENUE.

STEP 1 You need two items from **Income Statement**

Revenue generated from product sold	TOTAL REVENUE	$
Use **all direct costs** for producing goods	TOTAL COGS	$

STEP 2 Use the magic formula

Gross Margin = (Revenue – COGS)	$
Divide by Revenue	$
Multiply by 100	$
Gross Margin =	%

Tips to Improve Gross Margin 💡

- Increase Sales Prices: Consider adjusting your prices to better reflect the value of your products.

- Reduce Production Costs: Look for ways to cut costs in production, such as negotiating better prices for materials or improving production efficiency.

- Optimize Inventory: Manage your inventory effectively to reduce waste and ensure you're not overstocking or understocking.

PROFIT MARGIN

PROFIT MARGIN, ALSO KNOWN AS **NET PROFIT MARGIN**, REPRESENTS THE PERCENTAGE OF REVENUE THAT REMAINS AS PROFIT AFTER ALL EXPENSES ARE DEDUCTED.

STEP 1 You need two items from **Income Statement**

Net Profit minus all expenses from total revenue	NET PROFIT	$
This all monies made from sales	REVENUE	$

STEP 2 Use the magic formula

Net Profit	$
Divided by Revenue	$
Multiply by 100	$ |//
Profit Margin =	%

STEP 3 Interpret Results

High Profit Margin
🎉 Awesome! You're making a good profit from your sales.

Low Profit Margin
☹ Don't worry! You might need to find ways to reduce costs or increase sales prices.

RETURN ON EQUITY

RETURN ON EQUITY (ROE) IS A MEASURE OF A COMPANY'S PROFITABILITY IN RELATION TO SHAREHOLDERS' EQUITY.

STEP 1 You need two items from **Income Statement**

| Total profit after all expenses | NET INCOME | $ |
| All **shareholder's** hold in the company | EQUITY | $ |

STEP 2 Use the magic formula

Net Income = (Total Income - Total Expenses)	$
Divide by Shareholder's Equity	$
Multiply by 100	$
Return on Equity (ROE)	%

Tips to Improve Return on Equity

- Increase Net Income: Boost profitability through increased sales, cost reduction, and improving operational efficiency.

- Efficient Use of Equity: Ensure that investments and retained earnings are being used effectively to generate profit.

- Strategic Financial Decisions: Make informed decisions about reinvesting profits, paying dividends, or raising additional equity to maximize returns.

THIRD-QUARTER

Gross Profit Margin
Profit Margin
Return on Equity (ROE)

GROSS PROFIT MARGIN

GROSS MARGIN REPRESENTS THE PERCENTAGE OF REVENUE THAT EXCEEDS THE COST OF GOODS SOLD. IT INDICATES HOW WELL A COMPANY MANAGES ITS PRODUCTION COSTS RELATIVE TO ITS REVENUE.

STEP 1 You need two items from **Income Statement**

Revenue generated from product sold	TOTAL REVENUE	$
Use **all direct costs** for producing goods	TOTAL COGS	$

STEP 2 Use the magic formula

Gross Margin = (Revenue – COGS)	$
Divide by Revenue	$
Multiply by 100	$
Gross Margin =	%

Tips to Improve Gross Margin

- Increase Sales Prices: Consider adjusting your prices to better reflect the value of your products.

- Reduce Production Costs: Look for ways to cut costs in production, such as negotiating better prices for materials or improving production efficiency.

- Optimize Inventory: Manage your inventory effectively to reduce waste and ensure you're not overstocking or understocking.

PROFIT MARGIN

PROFIT MARGIN, ALSO KNOWN AS **NET PROFIT MARGIN**, REPRESENTS THE PERCENTAGE OF REVENUE THAT REMAINS AS PROFIT AFTER ALL EXPENSES ARE DEDUCTED.

STEP 1 You need two items from **Income Statement**

Net Profit minus all expenses from total revenue	NET PROFIT	$
This all monies made from sales	REVENUE	$

STEP 2 Use the magic formula

Net Profit	$
Divided by Revenue	$
Multiply by 100	$
Profit Margin =	%

STEP 3 Interpret Results

High Profit Margin
🎉 Awesome! You're making a good profit from your sales.

Low Profit Margin
😟 Don't worry! You might need to find ways to reduce costs or increase sales prices.

RETURN ON EQUITY

RETURN ON EQUITY (ROE) IS A MEASURE OF A COMPANY'S PROFITABILITY IN RELATION TO SHAREHOLDERS' EQUITY.

STEP 1 You need two items from **Income Statement**

Total profit after all expenses	NET INCOME	$
All **shareholder's** hold in the company	EQUITY	$

STEP 2 Use the magic formula

Net Income = (Total Income - Total Expenses)	$
Divide by Shareholder's Equity	$
Multiply by 100	$
Return on Equity (ROE)	%

Tips to Improve Return on Equity

- Increase Net Income: Boost profitability through increased sales, cost reduction, and improving operational efficiency.

- Efficient Use of Equity: Ensure that investments and retained earnings are being used effectively to generate profit.

- Strategic Financial Decisions: Make informed decisions about reinvesting profits, paying dividends, or raising additional equity to maximize returns.

FOURTH-QUARTER

Gross Profit Margin
Profit Margin
Return on Equity (ROE)

GROSS PROFIT MARGIN

GROSS MARGIN REPRESENTS THE PERCENTAGE OF REVENUE THAT EXCEEDS THE COST OF GOODS SOLD. IT INDICATES HOW WELL A COMPANY MANAGES ITS PRODUCTION COSTS RELATIVE TO ITS REVENUE.

STEP 1 You need two items from **Income Statement**

Revenue generated from product sold — TOTAL REVENUE $

Use **all direct costs** for producing goods — TOTAL COGS $

STEP 2 Use the magic formula

Gross Margin = (Revenue – COGS) $

Divide by Revenue $

Multiply by 100 $

Gross Margin =   %

Tips to Improve Gross Margin 💡

- Increase Sales Prices: Consider adjusting your prices to better reflect the value of your products.

- Reduce Production Costs: Look for ways to cut costs in production, such as negotiating better prices for materials or improving production efficiency.

- Optimize Inventory: Manage your inventory effectively to reduce waste and ensure you're not overstocking or understocking.

PROFIT MARGIN

PROFIT MARGIN, ALSO KNOWN AS **NET PROFIT MARGIN**, REPRESENTS THE PERCENTAGE OF REVENUE THAT REMAINS AS PROFIT AFTER ALL EXPENSES ARE DEDUCTED.

STEP 1 You need two items from **Income Statement**

Net Profit minus all expenses from total revenue	NET PROFIT	$
This all monies made from sales	REVENUE	$

STEP 2 Use the magic formula

Net Profit	$
Divided by Revenue	$
Multiply by 100	$
Profit Margin =	%

STEP 3 Interpret Results

High Profit Margin
🎉 Awesome! You're making a good profit from your sales.

Low Profit Margin
☹ Don't worry! You might need to find ways to reduce costs or increase sales prices.

RETURN ON EQUITY

RETURN ON EQUITY (ROE) IS A MEASURE OF A COMPANY'S PROFITABILITY IN RELATION TO SHAREHOLDERS' EQUITY.

STEP 1 You need two items from **Income Statement**

Total profit after all expenses	NET INCOME	$
All **shareholder's** hold in the company	EQUITY	$

STEP 2 Use the magic formula

Net Income = (Total Income - Total Expenses)	$
Divide by Shareholder's Equity	$
Multiply by 100	$
Return on Equity (ROE)	%

Tips to Improve Return on Equity

- Increase Net Income: Boost profitability through increased sales, cost reduction, and improving operational efficiency.

- Efficient Use of Equity: Ensure that investments and retained earnings are being used effectively to generate profit.

- Strategic Financial Decisions: Make informed decisions about reinvesting profits, paying dividends, or raising additional equity to maximize returns.

BALANCE SHEET RATIOS

Working Capital
Current Ratio
Quick Ratio
Debt Ratio

BALANCE SHEET

Assets		Amount ($)
Current Assets		
Cash and Cash Equivalents		20,000
Accounts Receivable		10,000
Inventory		15,000
Prepaid Expenses		2,000
Total Current Assets		**47,000**
Non-Current Assets		
Property, Plant, and Equipment (PP&E)		100,000
Less: Accumulated Depreciation		(10,000)
Total Non-Current Assets		**90,000**
Total Assets		**137,000**
Liabilities and Shareholders' Equity		
Current Liabilities		
Accounts Payable		8,000
Short-term Loans		10,000
Accrued Expenses		2,000
Total Current Liabilities		**20,000**
Non-Current Liabilities		
Long-term Debt		30,000
Total Non-Current Liabilities		**30,000**
Total Liabilities		**50,000**
Shareholders' Equity		
Common Stock		50,000
Retained Earnings		37,000
Total Shareholders' Equity		**87,000**
Total Liabilities and Shareholders' Equity		**137,000**

BALANCE SHEET BREAKDOWN

Assets

Total Current Assets: $20,000 (Cash and Cash Equivalents) + $10,000 (Accounts Receivable) + $15,000 (Inventory) + $2,000 (Prepaid Expenses) = $47,000

Total Non-Current Assets: $100,000 - $10,000 = $90,000

Total Assets: $47,000 (Total Current Assets) + $90,000 (Total Non-Current Assets) = $137,000

Liabilities and Shareholders' Equity

Total Current Liabilities: $8,000 (Accounts Payable) + $10,000 (Short-term Loans) + $2,000 (Accrued Expenses) = $20,000

Total Non-Current Liabilities: $30,000 (Long-term Debt) = $30,000

Total Liabilities: $20,000 (Total Current Liabilities) + $30,000 (Total Non-Current Liabilities) = $50,000

Total Shareholders' Equity: $50,000 (Common Stock) + $37,000 (Retained Earnings) = $87,000

Total Liabilities and Shareholders' Equity: $50,000 (Total Liabilities) + $87,000 (Total Shareholders' Equity) = $137,000

FIRST-QUARTER

Working Capital
Current Ratio
Quick Ratio
Debt Ratio

WORKING CAPITAL

UNDERSTANDING YOUR WORKING CAPITAL IS A KEY STEP IN MANAGING YOUR BUSINESS FINANCES. LET'S MAKE IT FUN AND EASY!

STEP 1 You need two items from **Balance Sheet**

TOTAL ASSETS

TOTAL LIABILITIES

STEP 2 Use the magic formula

Current Assets $

Minus Current Liabilities $

Working Capital $

STEP 3 Interpret Results

Positive Working Capital
🎉 Great job! You have enough assets to cover your liabilities.

Negative Working Capital
😟 Uh-oh! You might need to find ways to improve your cash flow or reduce your liabilities.

CURRENT RATIO

THE CURRENT RATIO MEASURES A COMPANY'S ABILITY TO PAY OFF ITS SHORT-TERM LIABILITIES WITH ITS SHORT-TERM ASSETS.

STEP 1 You need two items from **Balance Sheet**

Total profit after all expenses   CURRENT ASSETS

All **shareholder's** hold in the company   CURRENT LIABILITIES

STEP 2 Use the magic formula

Current Assets $

Divide by Current Liabilities $

Current Ratio =   %

Step 3 Interpret Results 📈

High Current Ratio: 🎉 Awesome! You have enough assets to cover your short-term liabilities.

Low Current Ratio: 😟 Don't worry! You might need to improve your asset management or reduce liabilities.

QUICK RATIO

THE QUICK RATIO, OR ACID-TEST RATIO, PROVIDES A MORE STRINGENT MEASURE OF LIQUIDITY BY EXCLUDING INVENTORY FROM CURRENT ASSETS.

STEP 1 You need two items from **Balance Sheet**

Total profit after all expenses	NET INCOME
All **shareholder's** hold in the company	EQUITY

STEP 2 Use the magic formula

Net Income = (Total Income - Total Expenses)	$
Divide by Shareholder's Equity	$
Multiply by 100	$
Return on Equity (ROE)	%

CASH RATIO

THE CASH RATIO IS THE MOST CONSERVATIVE LIQUIDITY RATIO, CONSIDERING ONLY CASH AND CASH EQUIVALENTS.

STEP 1 You need two items from **Balance Sheet**

CASH & CASH EQUIVALENTS	Liquid assets, including physical cash, bank balances, and short-term investments
CURRENT LIABILITIES	Obligations that need to be paid within one year.

STEP 2 Use the magic formula

Cash & Cash Equivalents	$
Divide by Current Liabilities	$
Multiply by 100	$
Cash Ratio =	%

STEP 3 INTERPRET YOUR RESULTS 📈

HIGH CASH RATIO: 🎉 FANTASTIC! YOU HAVE ENOUGH CASH TO COVER YOUR SHORT-TERM LIABILITIES.

LOW CASH RATIO: 😟 DON'T WORRY! YOU MIGHT NEED TO IMPROVE YOUR CASH RESERVES OR MANAGE LIABILITIES BETTER.

SECOND-QUARTER

Working Capital
Current Ratio
Quick Ratio
Debt Ratio

WORKING CAPITAL

UNDERSTANDING YOUR WORKING CAPITAL IS A KEY STEP IN MANAGING YOUR BUSINESS FINANCES. LET'S MAKE IT FUN AND EASY!

STEP 1 You need two items from **Balance Sheet**

TOTAL ASSETS

TOTAL LIABILITIES

STEP 2 Use the magic formula

Current Assets $

Minus Current Liabilities $

Working Capital $

STEP 3 Interpret Results

Positive Working Capital
🎉 Great job! You have enough assets to cover your liabilities.

Negative Working Capital
😟 Uh-oh! You might need to find ways to improve your cash flow or reduce your liabilities.

CURRENT RATIO

THE CURRENT RATIO MEASURES A COMPANY'S ABILITY TO PAY OFF ITS SHORT-TERM LIABILITIES WITH ITS SHORT-TERM ASSETS.

STEP 1 You need two items from **Balance Sheet**

Total profit after all expenses CURRENT ASSETS

All **shareholder's** hold in the company CURRENT LIABILITIES

STEP 2 Use the magic formula

 Current Assets $

 Divide by Current Liabilities $

 Current Ratio = %

Step 3 Interpret Results 📈

High Current Ratio: 🎉 Awesome! You have enough assets to cover your short-term liabilities.

Low Current Ratio: 😟 Don't worry! You might need to improve your asset management or reduce liabilities.

QUICK RATIO

THE QUICK RATIO, OR ACID-TEST RATIO, PROVIDES A MORE STRINGENT MEASURE OF LIQUIDITY BY EXCLUDING INVENTORY FROM CURRENT ASSETS.

STEP 1 You need two items from **Balance Sheet**

Total profit after all expenses	NET INCOME
All **shareholder's** hold in the company	EQUITY

STEP 2 Use the magic formula

Net Income = (Total Income - Total Expenses)	$
Divide by Shareholder's Equity	$
Multiply by 100	$
Return on Equity (ROE)	%

CASH RATIO

THE CASH RATIO IS THE MOST CONSERVATIVE LIQUIDITY RATIO, CONSIDERING ONLY CASH AND CASH EQUIVALENTS.

STEP 1 You need two items from **Balance Sheet**

CASH & CASH EQUIVALENTS	Liquid assets, including physical cash, bank balances, and short-term investments
CURRENT LIABILITIES	Obligations that need to be paid within one year.

STEP 2 Use the magic formula

Cash & Cash Equivalents	$
Divide by Current Liabilities	$
Multiply by 100	$
Cash Ratio =	%

STEP 3 INTERPRET YOUR RESULTS 📈

HIGH CASH RATIO: 🎉 FANTASTIC! YOU HAVE ENOUGH CASH TO COVER YOUR SHORT-TERM LIABILITIES.

LOW CASH RATIO: 😟 DON'T WORRY! YOU MIGHT NEED TO IMPROVE YOUR CASH RESERVES OR MANAGE LIABILITIES BETTER.

THIRD-QUARTER

Working Capital
Current Ratio
Quick Ratio
Debt Ratio

WORKING CAPITAL

UNDERSTANDING YOUR WORKING CAPITAL IS A KEY STEP IN MANAGING YOUR BUSINESS FINANCES. LET'S MAKE IT FUN AND EASY!

STEP 1 You need two items from **Balance Sheet**

TOTAL ASSETS

TOTAL LIABILITIES

STEP 2 Use the magic formula

Current Assets $

Minus Current Liabilities $

Working Capital $

STEP 3 Interpret Results

Positive Working Capital
🎉 Great job! You have enough assets to cover your liabilities.

Negative Working Capital
😟 Uh-oh! You might need to find ways to improve your cash flow or reduce your liabilities.

CURRENT RATIO

THE CURRENT RATIO MEASURES A COMPANY'S ABILITY TO PAY OFF ITS SHORT-TERM LIABILITIES WITH ITS SHORT-TERM ASSETS.

STEP 1 You need two items from **Balance Sheet**

Total profit after all expenses   CURRENT ASSETS

All **shareholder's** hold in the company   CURRENT LIABILITIES

STEP 2 Use the magic formula

Current Assets	$
Divide by Current Liabilities	$
Current Ratio =	%

Step 3 Interpret Results 📈

High Current Ratio: 🎉 Awesome! You have enough assets to cover your short-term liabilities.

Low Current Ratio: 😨 Don't worry! You might need to improve your asset management or reduce liabilities.

QUICK RATIO

THE QUICK RATIO, OR ACID-TEST RATIO, PROVIDES A MORE STRINGENT MEASURE OF LIQUIDITY BY EXCLUDING INVENTORY FROM CURRENT ASSETS.

STEP 1 You need two items from **Balance Sheet**

Total profit after all expenses	NET INCOME
All **shareholder's** hold in the company	EQUITY

STEP 2 Use the magic formula

Net Income = (Total Income - Total Expenses)	$
Divide by Shareholder's Equity	$
Multiply by 100	$
Return on Equity (ROE)	%

CASH RATIO

THE CASH RATIO IS THE MOST CONSERVATIVE LIQUIDITY RATIO, CONSIDERING ONLY CASH AND CASH EQUIVALENTS.

STEP 1 You need two items from **Balance Sheet**

CASH & CASH EQUIVALENTS	Liquid assets, including physical cash, bank balances, and short-term investments
CURRENT LIABILITIES	Obligations that need to be paid within one year.

STEP 2 Use the magic formula

Cash & Cash Equivalents	$
Divide by Current Liabilities	$
Multiply by 100	$
Cash Ratio =	%

STEP 3 INTERPRET YOUR RESULTS

HIGH CASH RATIO: FANTASTIC! YOU HAVE ENOUGH CASH TO COVER YOUR SHORT-TERM LIABILITIES.

LOW CASH RATIO: DON'T WORRY! YOU MIGHT NEED TO IMPROVE YOUR CASH RESERVES OR MANAGE LIABILITIES BETTER.

FOURTH-QUARTER

Working Capital
Current Ratio
Quick Ratio
Debt Ratio

WORKING CAPITAL

UNDERSTANDING YOUR WORKING CAPITAL IS A KEY STEP IN MANAGING YOUR BUSINESS FINANCES. LET'S MAKE IT FUN AND EASY!

STEP 1 You need two items from **Balance Sheet**

TOTAL ASSETS

TOTAL LIABILITIES

STEP 2 Use the magic formula

Current Assets $

Minus Current Liabilities $

Working Capital $

STEP 3 Interpret Results

Positive Working Capital
🎉 Great job! You have enough assets to cover your liabilities.

Negative Working Capital
😟 Uh-oh! You might need to find ways to improve your cash flow or reduce your liabilities.

CURRENT RATIO

THE CURRENT RATIO MEASURES A COMPANY'S ABILITY TO PAY OFF ITS SHORT-TERM LIABILITIES WITH ITS SHORT-TERM ASSETS.

STEP 1 You need two items from **Balance Sheet**

    Total profit after all expenses   CURRENT ASSETS

    All **shareholder's** hold in the company   CURRENT LIABILITIES

STEP 2 Use the magic formula

    Current Assets $

    Divide by Current Liabilities $

    Current Ratio =   %

Step 3 Interpret Results 📈

High Current Ratio: 🎉 Awesome! You have enough assets to cover your short-term liabilities.

Low Current Ratio: 😟 Don't worry! You might need to improve your asset management or reduce liabilities.

QUICK RATIO

THE QUICK RATIO, OR ACID-TEST RATIO, PROVIDES A MORE STRINGENT MEASURE OF LIQUIDITY BY EXCLUDING INVENTORY FROM CURRENT ASSETS.

STEP 1 You need two items from **Balance Sheet**

Total profit after all expenses	NET INCOME
All **shareholder's** hold in the company	EQUITY

STEP 2 Use the magic formula

Net Income = (Total Income - Total Expenses)	$
Divide by Shareholder's Equity	$
Multiply by 100	$
Return on Equity (ROE)	%

CASH RATIO

THE CASH RATIO IS THE MOST CONSERVATIVE LIQUIDITY RATIO, CONSIDERING ONLY CASH AND CASH EQUIVALENTS.

STEP 1 You need two items from **Balance Sheet**

CASH & CASH EQUIVALENTS	Liquid assets, including physical cash, bank balances, and short-term investments
CURRENT LIABILITIES	Obligations that need to be paid within one year.

STEP 2 Use the magic formula

Cash & Cash Equivalents	$
Divide by Current Liabilities	$
Multiply by 100	$
Cash Ratio =	%

STEP 3 INTERPRET YOUR RESULTS 📈

HIGH CASH RATIO: 🎉 FANTASTIC! YOU HAVE ENOUGH CASH TO COVER YOUR SHORT-TERM LIABILITIES.

LOW CASH RATIO: 😰 DON'T WORRY! YOU MIGHT NEED TO IMPROVE YOUR CASH RESERVES OR MANAGE LIABILITIES BETTER.

BE. SMART.

www.ingramcontent.com/pod-product-compliance
Lightning Source LLC
Chambersburg PA
CBHW082235220526
45479CB00005B/1244